Balsamic Vign

PGJackso

Introduction

I did a bit of an intro in the first book. Forget all that pretentious, 'what it says to me,' nonsense. Such things seem to be a bit on the attention seeking side. Just make of these words what you will.

I'd advise you to buy that first book though, if you haven't already (wink, wink. Winkey wink), and insert the intro here - mentally. Or just be mental. All good.

Oh, and before I forget. I avoid genre. Real creativity isn't hampered by following the rules.

Paul G Jackson
Nowhere warm or remarkable 2018

Opaque

Clarification expected in days
Best not disturb currently
I watch in the gloom
My impertinent ways
Awaiting that drink
How will you taste?
Another bubble
It sent out the scent
Like smoke Vulcan wrought
Perhaps I ought
To leave you alone
Just to clarify

Lavatorial Aroma

(I went to the toilet and it smelled like a dry cleaners)

It smells like ironed trousers
Dry damp bathroom fog
Caustic sweet aromas
This is illogical
Wrong for this environment
You know
This is my torment

Man Walking

Sweat covered hair
Greasy veneer
Unholy and rank
Blue damp anorak
Dirty spectacles
Dirty spectacle
Walk with authority
Sex symbol not
But in your mind
You fancy a lot
Fiction of self
Delusions
Delusion
Look like a pervert
Revert
To the young man you were
Yet
I won't

Never Again

Our father
Who art infernal
Shadows
Be thy fame
You don't exist
Your followers persist
To poison us
With their scam
Never again
In hell's imaginary flame
Would I serve suck a thing
That takes your money
Rapes your children
Whilst controlling everything
Religion the cheat
Worshiped by sheep
Slaughtered
By our father
Who art imaginary

She Looks

She looks so elegant
Fragile and slender
Those dark eyes of wisdom
Where playfulness dies

Though you try to impress
When doors are open
She glides like a goddess
Gracefully stroking her thighs

A smile that belies a mocking return
That burns like a jewel at your heart
Fingernails red with your blood
It's just in your dreams

She'll never be yours
She'll not even glance your way
But if you knew her
As well as you think

A different person resides
A let down
A fool
A disappointment again
Yet
She looks so elegant
False is her name
For shame
It's the same with us all

Who do we think we are?

Doomy Clouds

Darkness turns to lightness
The doomy clouds over the M8
Glasgow motorway hellish
Tired and need to rest

Lightness turns to half light
Heading to Perth and further
Dreading the A9 gloominess
Driving makes me depressed

Gas works to the left of me
Sewage to the right
Into the valley of dismal
Expect nothing. It's trite

Roads turn to streets
With roundabouts and bridges
Valleys and crap waterfalls
Nothing feels bright quite

Flashing sun through hillocks
Leafless trees bully brains
Cold and lifeless places
There are none of God's graces

Doomy clouds look down
Nature has a vile hatred
A certain kind of spite
Doomy clouds, all doomy clouds
Doomy clouds look down

And there

And there we go
Looking for answers
It doesn't matter
Life is brief
A whisper
A mist
A ghostly shadow
Formulas shatter
Death and grief
Vespers
Deist
And there we go
Off on the wrong foot
Tripped
Tripping
Fallen
A dim sun
Before the ache
For your sake
Don't think

Crocodile

I like tardigrades
Through heaven and through hell
Little piggy creatures
I like crocodiles as well
Tardigrades are tiny
Crocodiles are not
Tardigrades live
In extreme cold or hot
But not crocodiles

Alas!

(This is about the memory of a teacher from my school)

Alas!
Alias
An atlas
At last

He used to be a teacher
Stanley Banley Boo
But now he is at nowhere
Nothing much to do

Geographic
Class A7
Chaos
Chaos more

Am I a creature from the ark?
I'll knock your head
Off your shoulders
Chaos, chaos more

Alas!
It's crass
Chaotic mess
Long gone

Lost one summer
Then found in the mist
Snowball through window
Desk on the twist

Alas!
The vast

Crass past
Burnt atlas

A car of azure
Chalk in the road
Grazing thorns
The memory corrodes

Before I awoke
For age has arrived
Long to return
345 Knowing

Alas!
Alias
An atlas
At last

Alas!
It's crass
Chaotic mess
Long gone

A moment frozen and fading

Realise

'It's got to end'
I say as I wake up
Fitful sleep
Awake with horror

'It's got to end'
I'm walking along
Anxiety, grief
Perplexity, sorrow

'It's got to end'
It really must
I can't take this
Or live with it

'It's got to end'
But no one hears
No one cares
'Til noose tight fit

'It's got to end'
And so it goes
Swing side to side
Earth abides

I need to say 'goodbye'
To everyone I know
'It's got to end'
And so it goes

Religion

Turmoil
Turmoil
Who do you trust?
Religions with snake oil
They're not fussed
They'll make you their slave
They'll steal your thoughts
They'll substitute reality
With their nonsense you bought

Turmoil
Turmoil
It just bites hard
Consider the aftermath
Consider it all
All the answers
To questions in life
Must be a red flag
Doesn't seem right

Turmoil
Turmoil
Run like the wind
Escape mental prisons
That promise the Earth
Run

Millsong

Grist
Sounds corny
But there's trouble at t'mill
That reprobate within
An owl so Tawny
Missed
Powder and grain
Odorous refrain
Stored in sacks of twill
But still
They grind and grind
As if to find the spill
It's just a mist
You must trust this
An owl so Tawny
Missed
It flew away
Before ridding us
Of the prey

Vote Vetoed

Tick in the box
It's meaningless
The things we can change
We can't
A fix
A hoax
A running joke
Tick in the box
For nothing much
Things will change
If you cast your vote
Do you really think it true?
A fix
A hoax
A running jape
Tick in the box
For hope
A con
A scam
Diverts your attention
A fix
A hoax
A cruel joke
Tick in the box
Elect scum

Chantry Road Chertsey

Empty streets
No people
Just cars
This could be a ghost town
Yet an aroma
Tomato and onions

Silent streets
Just my ears
Hear the breeze
This could be a ghost town
Yet a bird flies
Over bare roofs

Empty places
A cat is all
So eerie
This could be a ghost town
The sun burns
My shadow moves

Empty streets
Ruination
Damnation
This could be a ghost town
Crumbling plaster
Suicide road

Frizzy

Frizzy blonde hair
You stand next to your car
Looking like you're surprised

Bare landscape
Bleak houses where you are
Depressed area I surmise

A life of drudge
Far from society
Left on the topsoil
Soulless void
Windswept and wet
Crumbling to death
The cold wind bites
You try to believe it's good

Through mud you slop
That earthy stink
You toil and toil
Soulless void
Windswept and dead
Crumbling with debt
The cold wind bites
No respite

I saw you
Just briefly

Abrazoz

Waters gently trickle
Birdsong fills the air
A busy anthill growing
Midst new mown grass
Fish that dart and shimmer
Surprise a waiting fox
All this was a moment
Beyond the looking glass

Text

Message by text
Or just a mess
Flat verbs
No feelings
Funny face
Demotivated by those words
Sarcastic
Narcissistic
Ironic or kind
Inverted parallax
Chews your head
Incontrovertible
Other worldly
Broody and burley
You depress me
Verbally possess me
I don't like it one bit
Misinterpreted
Inexpressive letters
Blank and emotionless
Have we lost our way?

Games

I think you probably get the gist
Nihilist
Disappointments gather clouds
As all around
Looks up and down
For reason cast
But not a hint in blue

I think you probably heard the rest
Existentialist
The mirror lies
It always lies
It tries to fool you
Ego provides
Your fate eschews

And There

There we are, all happy
Smiling like the cream is yours
Like the dream is yours
Avert your eyes, of course
I am one with nothing
Nothing is me
To a refined degree
And there it is
I woke up this morning knowing
This must stop
There we are, not happy
Knowing the end is in sight
Like the dream is an obscene blight
Happy
Fools
I am one with nothing
Nothing is me
To a defined degree
A divined degree
Happy
Fools
Throw down your tools
One day
A quiet day
We'll all give up

Monochromatic

Monochromatic
Totally fantastic
Power in plastic
Picture dramatic
Cathedrals pragmatic
Dogmatic catalyst
Capture the sun
Twixt dust in the attic

Villa

A lonely cry
Crying for a life to come
A life to come denied
Denied
The doctor said it's time
Face the end alone
Alone and frightened
Frightened
Looking back
But cannot reach and hold
Cannot hold back
Cannot pull it back
There is a distant star
Demise
A lonely cry
Then silence
Then ?

The Purple Dress

That shimmer and glitter
That's most refined
Purple and lushly plush
I have worshipped at your temple
Demure yet sensual
Features defined
Your presence causes hush
I have worshipped at your sanctuary
As a matter of fact, you see
I have worshipped at your shrine
The purple dress divine
It personifies you

Charisma

Charismatic preachers
American white teethies
Spout about what thou shalt
Imaginary world
Unicorns do not exist
But somehow their way does
"Give us all yer money
If you want to feel god's love"
Charismatic most asthmatic
No altruistic truth
Spew and spew
A lie for you they command
"Give us all yer money
If you want to feel god's hand"
"Give us all yer money
If you want to feel god's love"
"Give us all yer money"
Charismatic preachers
American white teethies
What a sham
Maleficent scum

I'm Not

I'm not quite sure I want to talk about this
I'm only sure of one thing
Or is it three?
In a tepid mood around you
Around the corner of life
One hundred and eighty degrees
Or is it just me?
That light you think is burning
It's gone away from here
A frosty visage colours me
It follows me to the end
A burning end
Or maybe not
I don't know
Where it's all gone I cannot imagine
They've stolen my soul

Your Holy books

Not for me
Though, every little counts
As I widdle into the sea
Not for me
I'd rather not read fiction
That's become social disease
Not for me
Why don't Unicorns exist?
Why not the Tooth fairy?
Not for me
Maybe for you
No irascible truism to deny
Not to decry
A tome to despise
Give hate a new epithet
Swaps love for hate
'Believe in God?
I'll kill you if it's not my God'
I heard the fool say
Not for me
No
Never for me
Don't taint the air with your imaginary friend in the sky
You won't blend in right
Not for me

Legends

Denizens of the deep
Dwellers of the brief world of thought
Imagine the life they have
Not real
Ghosts of the several seas
Kraken and creatures
Mythical dogmata in the mist they sought
What were we taught?
To sail the waves in boats of wood
Blown by winds
Leaving adulthood
Should be good
But
Doctored photographs
To keep the pretence
Sold for pennies
Worthless to retain

Garrulous Simon

Quarrelsome and opinionated
Opined in the clique
We never missed the point of your self-aggrandisement
You did
As if we were meant to worship a fool like you
Thinking you're so sensible
Garrulous in excremental expositions
Confident in boorishness
Reveal your inner pride
So superior in your own thoughts
I purport you were taught
By a corpse
That convinced you of your ego
Over bloated
Trouble at t' mill
You gormless creep
Shuffle back to Manchester
Jump in the canal
Put us out of your misery
I spit on your grave
I vomit on your tomb
I lament the womb that bore you
You bore, you

B E Parker

Cinematograph alters toward
Impart the knowledge
That's been transformed
From real to reel to lies
And more
I saw your face just 23
Disinterested before you died
So young to be
And yet so able
Bullets deadly fly
Why so foolish?
Why so young?
What demons in your mind?
Such foolish gold
Life on the road
You wore your wedding ring
Beautiful face
Damaged mind
Idiot children
Play your game
It reworks over time
This nonsensical paradigm
It's yours to own
Your terms were all denied
You were known

The Future

It's all so futile
My dear children
Couched in sepia verbiage
But surely it's a game
We are just amoebas
We happened upon land
Or so the legends say

It's all so futile
Our lives are short
Brief and totally worthless
A surly face presides
Fools decide
For nothing more than dust

It's all so futile
Pathetic struggling
Against all odds?
Just to die and be interned
In soil

You do the math or maths
Depending on what you learned
A learned friend
Speaks the same as me
But with a different bent
To be futile is destiny

My Purchase part 2

Gloop in carton
A plastic cartoon
Boiling water
Resurrecting what ought to
Be a snack
But looking back
It gave an acid attack
The last time
And
I beg your pardon

Too Late II

No one to hear my words
Those days are over
Gone the way of all my thoughts
Like dust that falls
In the path of light

All is broken sherds
I'm so tired out
Who would want this old mug?
Gone are the times
I ran out of trust

Like dust that falls
In the path of light

Nostalgic Reflex

Let me go back
Please
To that time when life was ahead
The time I drank pop instead
Of tea
Let me go back
Please
To see those people I loved
Asleep in their graves
Dead
Sadness
Unsuitable badness bequeathed to no one
Let me go back
Please
That I can recapture the vitality of youth
It may sound uncouth
But nativity in brevity
Was better than sexual encounter
A dirty book under the counter
Assuaged a teenage hunger
Younger
Apoplexy incongruous
It's absurd
Just, please
Let me go back
I miss those years
It's been too long
My memory plays tricks
Your name I can't recall
I just can't fix it
Can't quite see your face
Just a portrait on a headstone
Faded

Degraded
Weathered and worn
A remembrance unborn
Let me go back
I miss you all

Outside a Northern Hotel

Murky morning low sunlight
Rook caws like evil is here
Dark and light evolving in frost
Awake too early is a blight
Crusty eyelids open in fear
Steaming porridge makes me sick

Navy blue clouds a hint if sad red
Frozen windscreen won't defrost
Slipping underfoot is frustrating
Does it mean we endure so perplexed?
Like most
Berating and irritating

That feeling that everything's bleak
Seeing a twig in a wet yellow beak
The skies are not beautiful
Full of grey streaks
For the morning is terrible
Veritable unease

I am awake yet feel worn in the north

Too Late III

The shards of light
Altruistic and vain
Burn in my eyes
As I lay here

Tethered to a star
Embracing the dark
A world goes by
Impromptu with drear

A blade of free grass
Bombastic and proud
Point to the heavenly bright
Collecting the day within

Too late for the boy
Swept by the mushroom
That grows in Hiroshima now
Affecting a realm that spins

Oh bitter death bringers
Did you not understand?
No one here wants to go
Callously scarify Earth

I Phoned

Age of reason
Age of rage
Rage of season
Cage of God
This metal, plastic
Resin and glue
All that matters
In a phone to you
Barrage of questions
Someone's mad
Rage and reason
Against all odds
Heads all down
Walking around
Bumping into walls
Answering calls
We live connected
Yet lonely still
Cage of plastic
Makes us ill
I phone
You phone
He phoned me
Chase us around
The family tree

I Am

Eukaryote
Then carry out
Your DNA
Programming

From Then On

In the times of smoke and thunder
Driving horses into battle
A sword
A dirk
A helmet
In the dirt
An arm rose with a sword
Blood red like the rose
It froze in disbelief
How can we be so brutal?
Rape and loot all?
Is this right?
Battle clatter batter
Better than defeat
Fall at your feet
The forces are replete
With stories of murder
Is this right?
This tribal blight
This human trait to ruin
From then on
Not nobler
Just xenophobia
From then on
A curse

She Awaits

I sleep not
Yet rest
Cocooned in my world
Surrounded by treasures
At my behest
I collected
For years
No less
For years on end
Books occult
Arcane charms
Dusted
Covered
Coveted
I spy from my bed
The moon turns red
Full and carnal
She floats at my window
Entry granted
Flowing garments of black
Her quest
Why mention blood?
Dominatrix supreme
The bite is obscene
I love it
Need it
Orgasm of bleeding
She is feeding
Sensual feeling
Salacious and healing
It's obvious
Vampire makes Dampir
Night of lust

No disgust

Undead and supreme

Bed with no dreams

Come with me

Slum with me

Do vile things

That all those I tell

Will see what lust brings

I submit

I sleep not

Smoking in Bed

Darkness falls
In turmoil walls
Flaming curtain
One thing's certain
We need help

Burning floor
Exploding door
Cigarette dropped
In bed when propped
Fire house bell

Charred foam pillows
Smoke that billows
Smoking kills
Who pays the bills…..
…..for firemen?

Tattoo

Hoop in the ear
Blade through your rear
Needle in lip
It's just a blip
Skull over face
Marks that debase
Needlessly skips
To days of your youth
That mocks you in turn
As you turn to objects
Your memory burns
A tattoo so large
As big as a barge
It's bigger than you
Can this be artwork too?
Or is it madness?
Age sags the skin
Nose with a pin
A picture distorts
What were your thoughts
When you got that tattoo?
Was it really you?
Your pride and joy
Another twee folly
Cost you a penny
Much more
Age sags the will
Reduces the skill
A picture distorts
What were your thoughts
When you got that tattoo?
That tattoo
Was it really you?

Schopenhauer

Arthur sits at home with his dog
Mind in a fog
Of pessimism

Arthur thinks life disappoints
I see his point
Though shrill

Arthur died a long time ago
Was he peaceful though
In a Frankfurt flat?

I looked through his book case
Shopping an hour
If you really 'will'

Autumn Part 3b

A leaf fell
Autumn is well

Accosting the Mirage

The day continues
Humdrum
As usual
Patchy clouds fly
Undying
My perusal
Accosting the mirage

Spring

She wakes in the winter
Brings sun in her wake
To break the cold
I love you coiled
Awaiting return
Awaiting the birds
She is a season
Beautiful to face
Not a beautiful face
For she isn't real
Just a warming touch
After flowers look up
She wakes in winter
Breaking the spell
No erudite bale
That blows mist vail
Most effulgent I see
So welcome is she
Spring

DNA Part 4

My relatives hail from foreign climes
I have a large family tree
It is so vast
I have no room
For narrow minded bigotry

I have a bigger tree

17

I cannot see you
No matter how large
Sitting in the greenery
You wear camouflage

For Mark

(This is an in joke with a fellow poet where we discussed rhymes that are cliché)

Rhyme night
With light
City
With pretty
I agree
It's all fairly sh....(can't think of a rhyme).

These Long Years

He's gone these long years
It burns on the soul
That talent is extinguished
Forlorn
Tears
Needless waste
You made me laugh
You made me cry
Your presence effulgent
These long years
These long years
Disappear as we all will
Lugubrious thoughts
With no retort
These long years
Lost in a black hole
That brilliance diminished
Gone
These long years

Parisian Talk Flays

Peppermint walls surrounding
Smoke cascade smoke
Intellectual snobbery
Cloud of unknowing
Where this leads
I know not
Aluminium window frame
Moisture drips
In drops of cocaine
Thoughts are sewing
Where it leads
I sew not
Smooth dark wood doors
Worn dog hair carpet
Concrete parapet
Clouds of smoke blowing
Posing ego feeds
I glow not
Immortal words spoken
Ignore and ignore
Verbal in robbery
Pretentiousness going
Where this leads
I care not
But a world seeks approval
From vacuous people
Born from arrogance
Postulating arrogance
I defy you
Sepia seeping
Creeping and reaping no good
Gaze to horizon
What are your eyes on?

Nothing but fame
Attention seeking
Fools believing
Strutting nose in the air
Narcissistic stare
Stereotype in stilettos
Brown teeth bare
Unlovable
You
I defy you
Merely hollow
You

The Holy Roller

Preach your arrogant nonsense
Not just here
Scream at people in the street
Hate speech
Hate speech
More and more
You're replete
With love so fake
God is hate
Won't cure your illness
But
Will find your car keys
Won't talk to you
You pretend he does
Delusion hangs hard
Love me or hell looms
Gun to your head
It's your fault you're dead
Preach your arrogant nonsense
Not just here
Your god superior
Is psychotic and abusive
Slave driving conclusive
Preach your arrogant nonsense
Not just here
Dead ears

Resting

The slumber of kings
Is the slumber of all
Equally resting in pieces

Who do you worship
In man or machine?
The soil takes all to its end

Silence prevails
Over curtains of leaves
No matter the type or the species

Beneath snowy domes
You'd never really know
Who, why, what to defend

The slumber of kings
Proves their might was in vain
Who's afraid of the grave?

Carpet

They said she was like a carpet
They said she was a doormat
People always walked over her
Sadly that is simply that

Lip

A bloodied lip
Smashed by a brick
On heat soaked streets
A friend or foe
No more to know
Sore and aching
Energy fading
Out of breath
The sun burned wretch
Blistered skin
Form nemesis or kin
We all fall down
And this...
.....is sound!

Sago Saga

Anticipation
I gaze form the window
Where will I go when I've eaten my sago?
Winter coat that's a size too big
Boots that pinch my swollen cold feet
This degradation
I gaze from my vantage point
I point
There's no point
Where will I go when I've eaten my sago?
Poised at the door
Ready to say 'go'
Drifting in soft snow
Just eating my sago
Let's see how the day goes
Town gossips in the market
Sour faced and haughty
I don't think it's naughty
To snowball them today
I'll just eat my sago
Okay?

Peter is a Fool

It feels later than it is
Yet the stillness belies the rage
That burns within the heart of Armageddon
Imagination is one to accuse
Pale riders on
Horses that are ridden
By God's own bidding
Spitting his hate
Worship me or die
Love me or be killed
Narcissist in the sky
Not visible to the eye
But there
Or so many think
Peter is a fool
Who dares to deny?
A witch hunt ensues
If you don't believe in Armageddon
You sadden the acolyte
Fools speak with irrational spite
How dare you not believe?
Their Armageddon is real
In their own minds
Peter is a fool

Ribbon

You want my money
I see you in the street
Smiling brightly
Snare the unwitting
Charity needs me
Needs my money
But why do we live
In a society like this
The government should take care
But are to corrupt to bother
You want my money
When you smarmily greet
I look just slightly
But I'm not biting
I'll leave that to fleas
That bite your Mummy
But why do we live
In a society like this
The government should take care
But are to corrupt to bother
It's a game that's over too soon
A ribbon for this
A ribbon for that
All different colours
Sign up for internet
Phones or adopt a pet
Sorry
Not me
Not even slightly

Time

A bullet that flies
A blink of your eyes
The seasons go by
That's time
In the end we die

Salisbury Somewhere

Reaching for the sky are the hands
Spindly and grasping hands
Green to red to brown to gold
That cloak that falls to ground
Still the bones reach for the sky
Silhouettes in a winter scene
Ageless
Timeless
Growing unnoticed
Unless comparing photographs
Grasping hands
Hands upon hands
Gripping the soil
Beneath the surface
Made by surplus
Of the cloak they drop
Perch for a rook
Fed by a brook
Where sits a duck
Silhouettes in a winter scene
Ageless
Timeless
Flowing unnoticed
To you

PWD

My password to the door
A secret not deep
Forgotten by lovers
Far away

My personal comfort
A single word echoes
From deep within me
Every day

Emmsy

Emma Naughton-House
Resembles a hippopotamus
With rhetoric monotonous
Bores the spots off us

Wishing

I want to sit in a wing backed chair
Just staring at a log fire
Leadlight windows
Facing the shire
Shards of light
Framing floating particles
A vague respite
I deserve comfort now
It's only fair
I want to sit in a wing backed chair

Jimothy Winta

I feel contaminated
Your spite
Your life
I feel intimidated
Your filth
Your gripes

I feel so dominated
By fear
By hate
I feel

Awful

I feel like a homeless man
Beaten by police
I feel like the working class
Hated by the elites

I feel like the homeless in Windsor
When the royal wedding descended
Police insanity
Feeding the agenda
Psychopathic army grows

Anarchy Must Happen

Through the eyes of a child
A world to explore
To touch and remember
Ever more and more
It's a tour of the universe
Starting today
Colourful array
For the future
How funny

Through the eyes of an adult
The world to deplore
Society condemns you
Unless you conform
It's the bore of the universe
Powers hold sway
They'll blow you away
For their pleasure
And money

Suited rich men
Plastic surgery whores
All we deplore
But they rule us
The media commands us
To think as they think
To kill those disobeying
To a different god praying
Wake up people
This world is corrupt

Ghost

Tattered winged beast
Peripheral vision spied
Black
Ashen of ashes
Brash and sneering a lie
Shadowy
Not of this world
Floating eerily by
Overhead
A laughing chimera
I saw you
I saw you
I did
I saw you
Drifting ghost over the fields
Right in front
Red sky aglow
I saw you go
You saw me
But ignored me
It's making me panic
How real are you?
It's beyond sanity
Clad so meagrely
In a death mask
Flying regally
I saw you
Implore you
Get well away
Don't lead me to Hades today
Gates of fire
You'll have my soul
I bid thee

Go away
I saw you
I saw you
Another realm dreams
But here I cannot hold on
I'm drifting away
Like opiate haze
Is calling me
Calling me on
I saw you
I saw you
I did
I saw you
Drifting ghost over the fields
Ghost over the fields
Over the fields
The fields
Fields

Food Poisoning?

Vertigo
Nausea
In my throat
Watery tongued responses
Belly bloats
Stabbing pain
Again and again
Careless steps
Fever breaks
My sense ensconces
Soiled carpet
Too late
Too late
Regret

Traffic Light in a bin bag

The tattered cloak
Phantom bespoke
Dancing in the wind
Malevolence underpinned
Flying twisted corpse
What do you purport?

Headless
Heedless
Inanimate fixture
Traffic
Sarcastic shtick
Relentless forward
Ignoring the ghost
Over-self morose
Travelling standstill
Battling windmill
Faceless
Baseless terror

Augenblick
Krótko
Just a moment
Just in a moment
One just moment
I saw you
You blinked away to nothing
I was wrong
I refer to 'Villa'
Can you find me?
Can you fault me?
Can you see the wind?
Is it wrong to be frightened?

Is it frightening to be wrong?
Wear the tattered cloak
A black coat bespoke
Swaying in the squall
Unkindness reinforced
Flying twisted corpse
What do you sense?
Fear intense

Helpdesk

Oh, Hi. Yes.
Difficulty
All gone wrong
Loud voices
Laughing teeth
Obviously

Oh, Hi. Yes.
Difficulty
Too far flung
Activities
Written in brief
Odiously

Oh, Hi. Yes.
Difficulty
You know the rest
Feeling stressed
Just having kittens
The theif

Oh, Hi. Yes.
Difficulty
Lack of answers
Unacceptable
Can have a look
Once bitten

Today was the day

Today it arrived
Dusty box
Monolith shaped
Containing much
Wooden delight
Sore eyes a sight

Today it arrived
Cut the box
Bubble wrap draped
Zipped in a case
Strings and knobs
Awkwardly lobs

Plays like a dream
Loud and extreme
Gone for a song
Bargain supreme

But wait
Damp will warp
The reddened board
Joyless now

Rain Always

Rain
Rain
Always rain
Like all that water
Soaks night porter
Rain
It's always rain
One summer
Brighton beach
Running fleet
Dancing feet
Then rain
Summer glasshouse
Black Crombie
Green Parka
Wet shoes
Rain
Rain

Jim of Plastic Street

Beast of burden
Burden of proof
Kowtowing cow
Not cloven hoof
Fifteen in space
Spaces between
Prognostication
Abstractionism
Jimmy a Plastic
Beast of burden

Are Ruler

They sent him
To cause chaos
This mug cannot see it
Political emoluments
Dung breath and uncouth

They sent him
Causing confusion
Obfuscate reality
Keep the people busy
They'll never see the truth

They call him
'Are ruler'
A simple folk are they
That eat the filth they're told to
Brainless beyond belief

Pix

What a grotty photograph
Yet the scene looked just ideal
It's dark and blurred
It's reeking stench
It's burning in the bin

What a fine scene in the wild
The sun is lighting all
It can exact
A certain flow
Please no pictures here

Oh, Hell!

Stress is caused by other people
Especially family ties
Let downs all prevail
Yet, I tell not lies

Indifferent to your inner feelings
They fight you with no regard
Oblivious of the stress effect
No hope within the mirage

Stress is caused by other people
Impacting on your feelings
If they would look with empathy
They'd stop their foolish reeling

Stress is caused by other people
Primitive in their thoughts
Stress is caused by other people
No other retort

TV Lies

TV is so boring
American or UK
Nothing seems to 'wow' me
Same old same old same

Cinema predictable
Some blokes have a fight
Some slag will strut her stuff
Tropes that aren't too bright

That same old formulaic stuff
The stories have nothing new
A lone American wins the war
Or losing fighter pulls through

LAPD against all odd
A white cop wins the day
Single handed, as you'd expect
Happily ever after
Averts worldwide disaster

Actual life is different
No hero on the streets
In reality
Corrupt coppers beat up children
Bludgeon old ladies to death
When no one's beholding
And they'll get away with it
Hidden behind their uniform
That's the reality of being
TV is so boring
Real life is hatred from authority
Your leaders are scroungers

Scum that has risen
I laugh in derision
At them
Pampered and worshiped
May death be their throne
Cut their throats
But
TV is so boring
American or Brit
Nothing seems to 'wow' me
Same old same old same
A load of old……………..

Helden

I have no heroes
Like once I did
Like TV showed me
The newspapers print

I have no heroes
They're just like me
Sweating in heat
Ungainly not twee

I have no heroes
Leave me alone
They all become failures
Disappointing again

I laugh in derision
As some kiss your feet
Inelegant buffoons
I spit, I spit

Beautiful angel
Time doth erode
The wild wind blows
Heroes to scald

Game Your

What is this life
So full of commercials?
Paper and plastic
Metal, controversial
Someone is begging
Beleaguered
Skin shedding
Underdog barking
Overdog laughing
This is your world
A game
A game
A game
Again
Worse than the Matrix
A world of false reason
Yet we readily conform
It's merely the norm
We haven't yet spoken
We haven't awoken

Brook

From left to right
A hubbub
A glisten
The sound of the brook
Then only to look

From fallen branch
An insect
Crawling
Profound overlooked
The sound of the brook

Muddy shoes
Squashing
Sinking
A perfect delirium
Yet depressing as well

Two people meet
A lover a fool
Swept away
Deceptive they say
By the water
Near a tree
From left to right
Expressing so well
The feelings within
So veiled
So thin
A hubbub
Crawling

Down in the forest

A brook trickles on
What stories to tell
But never can

Twilight begins
From left to right
Forgetting the time

The tree will die
As love will die
The water rolls along
The brook is your song

A Theist

That look of indifference
God gave to me
Almost as if
My name is Godfree

Spikes

I
Am
Not
Fine
Above
Mizzly
Piazzas

A
Go
Now
Mind
Alive
Simmers

Perish the thought

The man I was has perished
Forlorn and long ago
A time I wore a white shirt
Ironed, washed hair blown

There was a feeling once
It seems to dissipate
That I once had a life
Love would reciprocate

I have made many mistakes
The main one was to live
Oblivious of reality
Please forgive and give

The man I was is fading
More tired every hour
A headstone is my future
I rest beneath the flowers

There is a field afar
A place where I can go
To rest with my ancestors
There is no Hell below

No Heaven in the clouds
It's all a grand delusion
Nothing good or bad awaits
When I leave this desolation

The man I was has perished
Forlorn horizon bound
A headstone is my future

No light, not even sound

A headstone is my future
A headstone for my thoughts
Perish those immaculate things
A headstone I have bought

Illness

Hot but cold
Floored yet bored
Include the ceiling
Into the fold

Water, yes, water
Watery eyes
Time never dies
But we do

Of nothing
Tiny little germ
It wriggled right inside of me
I squirm

Amsterdam pancakes
Westermarkt
I wish I was there
Instead of dying
Do you?

Hope You're Well

Hope you're well
In rude health
The ruder the better
Rude Boy skank

Hope you're well
This letter requests
Your company soon
Rasta top rank

Hope you're well
In city walled hell
Where fools all dream
It's getting better

Hope your well
Is full of clean water
To cleanse your soul
And wash your Lambretta

Looking Up

A final dream
To end my day
That clouds be home
Where dragons lay

Where children play
When I was young
Innocent
Idyllic day

Other titles in paperback by the author:

Balsamic Vignette : Poetry

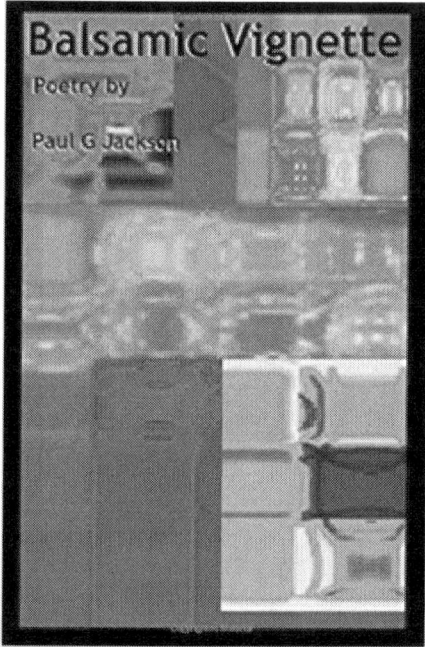

Boomshot : Adult only content. Novel

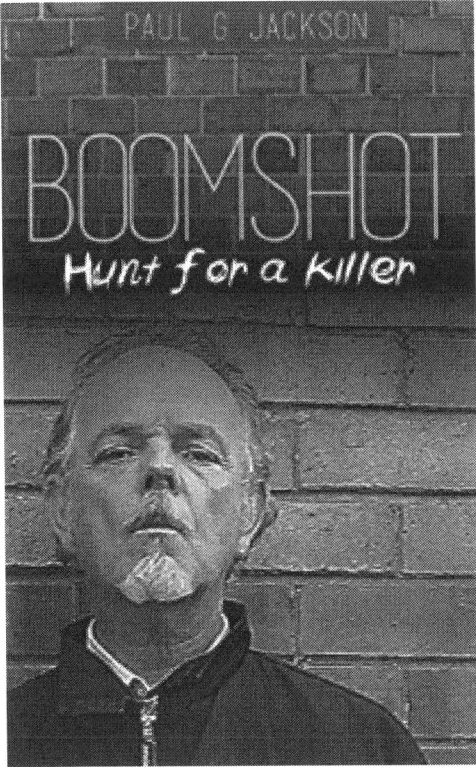

The Jumbly Jungle Tales : Humour

The Tortured Pen : Mixed genre. Includes Adult only short stories

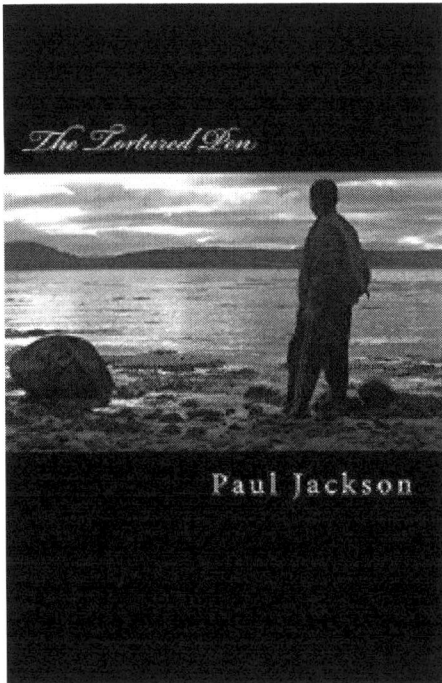

Tales from a Lonely Life : Mixed genre short stories

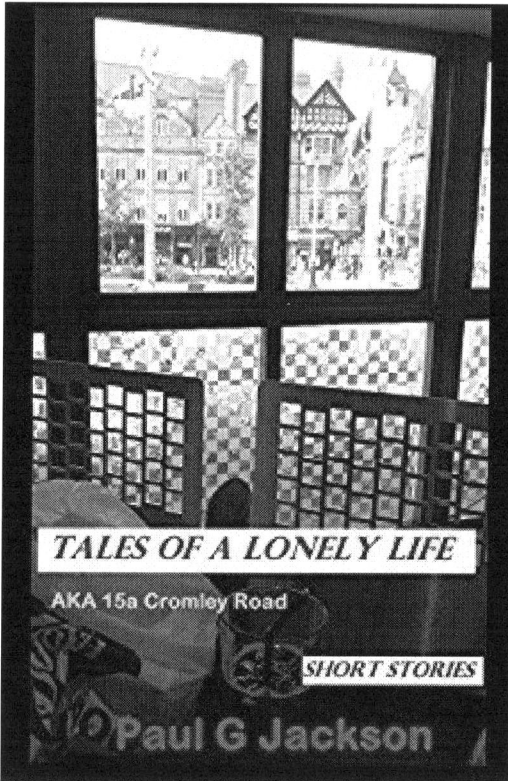

End word

Plop

There was a young man from Rome
That sat on the porcelain throne
He grunted and stressed
For hours depressed
All he released was a groan

Made in the USA
Columbia, SC
29 June 2018